# Reading

## PRACTICE QUESTIONS

Laura Collinson

RISING STARS

## Acknowledgements

Rising Stars is grateful to the following schools who will be utilising Achieve to prepare their students for the National Tests: Chacewater Community Primary School, Cornwall; Coppice Primary School, Essex; Edgewood Primary School, Notts; Henwick Primary School, Eltham; Norwood Primary School, Southport; Sacred Heart Catholic Primary School, Manchester; Sunnyfields Primary School, Hendon; Tennyson Road Primary School, Luton.

### Photo credits

Photos from iStock: p6 pigeon © soleg; p8 balai de paille © meailleluc; p10 lamp © Timoxa33; p22 sun © Robin_Hoood; p26 snail © Avalon_Studio; p28 liquorice © MaximShebeko; p32 leaves © Peterfactors; p34 giraffe © kotomiti; p38 orang-utan © GlobalP; p40 chocolate bar © sumnersgraphicsinc; p48 pumpkin © nelik; p52 moon © WestLight; p54 centipede © Alasdair Thomson p28 Waggon © Beamish, the living museum of the North

### Text extracts

p6 Pigeon Summer © 1992 Ann Turnbull. Reproduced by permission of Walker Books Ltd, London SE11 5HJ www.walker.co.uk; p10 A Sudden Puff of Glittering Smoke by Anne Fine. Published by Egmont; p12 From My Story: Anne Boleyn and Me © Alison Prince, 2004. Reproduced by permission of Scholastic Ltd. All rights reserved; p16 An Elephant in the Garden © 2011 Michael Morpurgo. Reprinted by permission of HarperCollins Publishers Ltd; p18 The Magician's Nephew by C.S. Lewis © C.S. Lewis Pte. Ltd. 1955. Extract reprinted by permission; p20 Stig of the Dump by Clive King published by Puffin 1993; p22 First Puffin Picture Book of Stories from World Religions by Annabel Shilson-Thomas, illustrated by Barry Smith. (Puffin Books, 1996) Text © Annabel Shilson-Thomas, 1996. Illustrations © Barry Smith, 1996; p24 image and text © Beamish, The Living Museum of the North; p28 Boy – Tales of Childhood by Roald Dahl, published by Jonathan Cape Ltd & Penguin Books Ltd. Also reprinted by permission of Farrar, Straus, and Giroux, LLC. All Rights Reserved; p32 'Colour Your Autumn' article © National Trust; p34 Whipsnade zoo article © Whipsnade Zoo; p36 'Jacqueline Wilson at Christmas' © The Mail on Sunday/Event Magazine; p38 'The orang-utan nursery' © Daily Mail; p40 'The History of Chocolate' © Primary Times; p44 'The Sound Collector' and p46 'The Reader of this poem' Reprinted by permission of Peters Fraser & Dunlop (www.petersfraserdunlop.com) on behalf of Roger McGough; p48 'Pumpkin for Maxine' from Two's Company by Jackie Kay; p50 'Me and my brother' by Michael Rosen; p52 'Silver' by Walter de la Mare; p54 'The centipede's song' from James and the Giant Peach by Roald Dahl, published by Penguin Books Ltd.

Every effort has been made to trace all copyright holders, but if any have been inadvertently overlooked, the Publishers will be pleased to make the necessary arrangements at the first opportunity.

Although every effort has been made to ensure that website addresses are correct at time of going to press, Rising Stars cannot be held responsible for the content of any website mentioned in this book. It is sometimes possible to find a relocated web page by typing in the address of the home page for a website in the URL window of your browser.

Hachette UK's policy is to use papers that are natural, renewable and recyclable products and made from wood grown in sustainable forests. The logging and manufacturing processes are expected to conform to the environmental regulations of the country of origin.

ISBN: 978 1 78339 544 6

© Rising Stars UK Ltd 2015

First published in 2015 by Rising Stars UK Ltd, part of Hodder Education, an Hachette UK Company
Reprinted 2015

Carmelite House

50 Victoria Embankment

London EC4Y 0DZ

www.risingstars-uk.com

Author: Laura Collinson

Series Editor: Helen Lewis

Accessibility Reviewer: Vivien Kilburn

Publishers: Kate Jamieson and Laura White

Project Manager: Estelle Lloyd

Editorial: Sarah Davies, Rachel Evans, Anne Kilraine, Fiona Leonard

Additional questions written by Maddy Barnes (p9, q1; p11, q2; p13, q2; p15, q1, 2; p19, q3; p23, q2; p25, q1; p29, q2; p33, q2; p33, q2; p39, q4; p45, q5; p55, q1)

Cover design: Burville-Riley Partnership

Illustrations by David Burroughs and John Storey

Text design and typeset by the Pen and Ink Book Company Ltd

Printed by the Gutenberg Press, Malta

A catalogue record for this title is available from the British Library.

# Contents

## Fiction

## Non-fiction

## Poetry

*The answers can be found in a pull-out section in the middle of this book.*

*Welcome to Achieve Key Stage 2 Reading Practice Questions 100*

In this book you will find lots of practice and information to help you achieve the expected scaled score of 100 in the Key Stage 2 Reading test.

It contains lots of reading extracts, some fiction, some non-fiction and some poetry. Each extract is followed by a selection of questions testing different reading skills, such as comprehension, making inferences, making predictions and the effect of language choices on meaning.

# About the Key Stage 2 Reading National Test

The test will take place in the summer term in Year 6. It will be done in your school and will be marked by examiners – not by your teacher.

In the test you will be given a booklet containing a range of texts and another booklet for your answers. The texts will be from a range of fiction, non-fiction and poetry. The first text will be the easiest and the last text will be the most challenging. The texts and questions will be very similar to the texts that you have been reading in school. You will have one hour to read the texts and complete the answer booklet.

The test is worth a total of 50 marks.

- Some questions ask you to find the answer in the text. These questions are usually worth 1 mark. These make up 44–66% of the marks.
- Some questions ask you to write a short answer. These questions are usually worth 2 marks. They make up 20–40% of the marks.
- Other questions ask you to write a longer answer. These are worth 3 marks. They make up 6–24% of the marks.

# Test techniques

## Before the tests

- Try to revise little and often, rather than in long sessions.
- Choose a time of day when you are not tired or hungry.
- Choose somewhere quiet so you can focus.
- Revise with a friend. You can encourage and learn from each other.
- Read the 'Top tips' throughout this book to remind you of important points in answering test questions.
- KEEP READING all kinds of non-fiction, fiction and poetry texts.

## During the tests

- READ THE QUESTION AND READ IT AGAIN.
- If you find a question difficult to answer, move on; you can always come back to it later.
- Always answer a multiple-choice question. If you really can't work out the answer, have a guess.
- Check to see how many marks a question is worth. Have you written enough to 'earn' those marks in your answer?
- Read the question again after you have answered it. Check you have done what the question asked you to do.
- If you have any time left at the end, go back to the questions you have missed. If you really do not know the answers, make guesses.

# Pigeon summer

These questions will help you practise:
* ★ understanding words in context
* ★ identifying how language choices enhance meaning
* ★ summarising main ideas
* ★ making comparisons
* ★ identifying key details
* ★ making predictions.

'Get the washing in, for heaven's sake!' snapped Mum. She thrust the basket at Mary. 'Couldn't you have grabbed it when it started to rain? Standing there gawping up at those birds. You never *think*.'

She went in, slamming the door.

Mary snatched the pegs from the line, tossing the clothes unfolded into the basket. They had been damp anyway, but they were getting rapidly wetter as she worked her way along. The rain soaked into the shoulders of her cardigan and trickled down the back of her neck.

The line cleared, she backed in through the door with the heavy basket. Her mother was ironing.

'Hang them round the fire,' she said.

Mary began draping towels and nappies over the rack.

'You never think,' said Mum again. 'There's Phyl putting Lennie to bed, and I had Doreen, and what are you doing? Standing out in the rain staring up at those blasted pigeons.'

She banged the iron down, folded a pillowcase and picked up a blouse. Mary hung the last nappy on the rack. 'I've got to shut them away,' she said.

'Yes, and when you've done that you can take this lot upstairs,' said Mum.

Mary went to the door.

'The washing was wet any road,' she said, and flounced out before her mother could answer. She was angry because she knew she should have noticed; somehow she could never do anything right for her mother.

Ann Turnbull

**1** *Standing there gawping up at those birds.*

What does the word *gawping* mean in this sentence?

Tick **one**.

reaching ☐

staring ☐

listening ☐

talking ☐

**2** **Find** and **copy** the word that tells the reader that Mum doesn't like the pigeons.

_____

**3** Number the events from **1** to **4** in the order they happen in the text.

Mary hung the washing by the fire. ☐

Mary went outside to shut the pigeons away. ☐

Mary's mum did the ironing. ☐

Mary's mum thrust the washing basket at Mary. ☐

**4** How are Mary's actions different compared to those of her sister, Phyl?

_____

_____

_____

**5** The text suggests that Mary's mum is cross with her.
Give **two** details to support this idea.

1. _____

2. _____

**6** What do you think Mary's mum will do now that Mary has walked out of the house?
Explain your answer with reference to the text.

_____

_____

_____

# The wind in the willows

These questions will help you practise:
★ retrieving and recording information
★ identifying key details
★ explaining the meaning of words in context
★ identifying how language choices enhance meaning
★ explaining inferences.

The Mole had been working very hard all the morning, spring-cleaning his little home. First with brooms, then with dusters; then on ladders and steps and chairs, with a brush and a pail of whitewash; till he had dust in his throat and eyes, and splashes of whitewash all over his black fur, and an aching back and weary arms. Spring was moving in the air above and in the earth below and around him, penetrating even his dark and lowly little house with its spirit of divine discontent and longing. It was small wonder, then, that he suddenly flung down his brush on the floor, said, 'Bother!' and 'O blow!' and also, 'Hang spring-cleaning!' and bolted out of the house without even waiting to put on his coat. Something up above was calling him **imperiously**, and he made for the steep little tunnel which answered in his case to the gravelled carriage-drive owned by animals whose residences are nearer to the sun and air. So he scraped and scratched and scrabbled and **scrooged**, and then he scrooged again and scrabbled and scratched and scraped, working busily with his little paws and muttering to himself, 'Up we go! Up we go!' till at last, pop! his snout came out into the sunlight, and he found himself rolling in the warm grass of a great meadow.

'This is fine!' he said to himself. 'This is better than whitewashing!' The sunshine struck hot on his fur, soft breezes caressed his heated brow, and after the seclusion of the **cellarage** he had lived in so long, the carol of happy birds fell on his dulled hearing almost like a shout. Jumping off all his four legs at once, in the joy of living and the delight of spring without its cleaning, he pursued his way across the meadow till he reached the hedge on the further side.

Kenneth Grahame

## Glossary

- **imperiously** bossily
- **scrooged** dug
- **cellarage** several underground rooms

**1** Circle the correct option to complete the sentence below.

When Mole jumped out into the meadow he felt…

| revitalised. | bored. | scared. | dirty. |

**2** How do you know that Mole would rather be above ground than do the cleaning?
Write **two** details that support this.

1. _____

2. _____

**3** *Spring was moving in the air above and in the earth below and around him, penetrating even his dark and lowly little house.*

Explain why the word *penetrating* is a suitable word to use for spring.

_____

**4** **Find** and **copy** the phrase that refers to other animals' homes.

_____

**5** The writer has used **alliteration** in this text.

**Find** and **copy one** example to show this.

_____

**6** Why do you think Mole was so keen to leave his home and go above ground?

Explain fully and refer to the text in your answer.

_____
_____
_____
_____
_____

# A sudden puff of glittering smoke

These questions will help you practise:
★ retrieving and recording information
★ explaining how meaning is enhanced through choice of words
★ identifying how information is related
★ giving / explaining the meaning of words in context
★ making and explaining inferences.

'Who can name somewhere else really hot?' asked Mr Piper.

'Where are you from?' Jeanie whispered to the genie.

'Baghdad,' he replied, idly crossing one leg over the other and picking at a loose thread in his silver slipper. 'It was the shining jewel of all Arabia.'

'Baghdad!' called out Jeanie, and added without thinking, 'It was the shining jewel of all Arabia.'

Mr Piper's eyes widened.

'Well done! And can you tell us anything more about it?' She glanced down at the genie, still lazing on the desk. Could she?

The genie smiled. Then, gently, he blew. A stream of glittering mist flew up from his mouth and swirled around Jeanie like rings around a planet.

'In the good old days,' she heard herself saying, 'Baghdad was truly a city of marvels. Mere words cannot describe its mysteries or its wonders.'

Everyone stared. Mr Piper's mouth dropped open. The genie shut his eyes till his dark lashes fluttered on his cheeks, and blew and blew, and Jeanie began to speak of the most magnificent palace from which four highways ran out through massive gateways in high walls, and stretched to the corners of the old Arab empire. She spoke of merchants travelling east and west, and of enormous wealth and terrible poverty. She used words she had never used before – words she had never even heard! She told them about the ruler – Caliph, she called him. She told them about mosques made of finely patterned tiles where Muslims gathered to worship Allah. She spoke of vast bazaars humming with people buying and selling.

'Jeanie!' cried Mr Piper. 'You must have spent the whole weekend locked in the library, to know so much!'

Jeanie tried to stop. But the genie still blew. The glittering rings still circled round her head. Without wanting to keep on, she found herself telling Mr Piper all about houses built of sun-dried bricks, white-washed to hurl the heat of the fierce sun back in its face. She told him about cool hidden courtyards and wooden shutters that kept out the sun by day and the desert winds by night.

Anne Fine

**1** a) To what does the writer compare the mist from the genie's mouth?

_____

b) What is the effect of making this comparison?

_____

_____

**2** **Find** and **copy** the group of words that show Jeanie is about to refer to information about the past.

_____

**3** **Find** and **copy two** details to show how the genie continued to provide Jeanie with the answers to the question.

1. _____

2. _____

**4** What does the phrase _hurl the heat_ mean in the final paragraph?

_____

_____

**5** Why do you think Mr Piper's eyes _widened_ when Jeanie described Baghdad as _the shining jewel of all Arabia_?

_____

_____

_____

# A Tudor girl's diary

These questions will help you practise:
★ retrieving and recording information
★ making inferences
★ identifying key details
★ explaining inferences
★ summarising main ideas from a text.

### 18th May 1536

The swordsman is not here yet because he was delayed on the road from Dover. A man who came here with a message for the King told us the Queen was distressed to hear of the delay. The execution was set for this morning, and she had hoped it would be over by now. The man said the Constable of the Tower assured her there would be no pain, and she laughed and put both hands round her slender throat, saying she had only a little neck.

I wish I did not have to hear such details. Like everyone else, I have seen many executions, and always thought nothing of them, but it is different when I know the condemned prisoner so well. I might have been in her place, had our paths followed different ways. I cannot stop thinking about her. I keep remembering the moment when she leaned her head towards me in need of comfort. I wish now that I had responded.

Ever since the death sentence, Henry has been behaving with a gaiety that most of us find distasteful. Perhaps he does not want to be alone with his conscience. Whatever the reason, he has plunged into constant parties and celebrations, with musicians playing and much feasting and drinking. I myself have been summoned several times to play for him. I reminded him yesterday that I am officially dismissed, but he just shrugged his heavy shoulders. Music, he said, speaks more sweetly than words.

### 19th May 1536

It is over. Anne Boleyn, Queen of England, died this morning at nine o'clock. The King did not witness her execution, and neither did the Duke of Norfolk. I was there with Mama. She insisted on seeing the end of 'that woman' – for the sake of Queen Catherine, she said. Tom kept the children in the **smithy** with him. They always like the smoke and the clanging iron and the patient horses.

The time of the execution was supposed to be a secret, but a huge crowd of people had crammed onto the green in the centre of the Tower. The scaffold had been built high, so that everyone could see, and it was draped with black cloth and scattered with straw. The heavy wooden block stood in the centre, with a lot of straw at its base. The executioner wore black clothes, with a hood that covered his head and a mask over his face, as if he was taking part in some grim carnival. There was no sword in his hand, and a man beside me said it was hidden in the pile of straw behind him. He was right – when I looked carefully I could see the hilt sticking out. A priest stood ready, murmuring prayers.

From *My Story: Anne Boleyn and Me* by Alison Prince

 **Glossary**

• **smithy** blacksmith's workshop where iron tools and horseshoes are made

**1** Why was the execution delayed?

_____

_____

**2** Using information from the text, tick **true** or **false** in the following table.

|  | True | False |
|---|---|---|
| The swordsman was late. |  |  |
| Henry has been behaving in a distressed manner. |  |  |
| Anne Boleyn died at seven o'clock. |  |  |
| The executioner's head was covered. |  |  |

**3** Why do you think the children were kept in the smithy?

_____

_____

**4** The text suggests that Henry was not upset by the beheading. Give **two** reasons to support this idea.

1. _____

2. _____

**5** The writer mentions _Mama_. What is Mama's opinion of the Queen?
Use evidence from the text to support your answer.

_____

_____

_____

**6** Think about what happens in this diary entry.
Write a headline for a newspaper article about these events.

_____

# A midsummer night's dream

These questions will help you practise:
★ retrieving and recording information
★ explaining the meaning of words in context
★ identifying key details
★ making inferences
★ making predictions.

## Act 1

(*Theseus' palace*)

**Egeus**: My lord, my daughter Hermia wants to marry Lysander but I want her to marry this fine man, Demetrius.

**Theseus**: Then as you wish, Demetrius it must be.

**Egeus**: Thank you, my lord.
(*Exit Demetrius and Egeus.*)

**Hermia**: But I cannot marry Demetrius when it is you who I love, Lysander!

**Lysander**: Let's run away tonight. We will go through the forest to my aunt's house and get married.

**Hermia**: Yes! Let's meet later at the city gate.

**Lysander**: Until then, goodbye my love.
(*Exit Lysander. Enter Helena.*)

**Helena**: Why are you so happy Hermia?

**Hermia**: I am going to run away tonight to marry my love, Lysander.

**Helena**: Lucky you! (*aside*) I will tell Demetrius to make him jealous. Perhaps that way I'll win his heart.

## Act 2

(*Enter the Mechanicals. They mime working in their shops.*)

**Snug**: Closing time! (*Everyone stops and gathers together.*)

**Quince**: I'm Peter Quince, a carpenter and playwright. Is everyone here?

**Bottom**: Nick Bottom the weaver here!

**Starveling**: Robin Starveling the tailor here!

**Snug**: Snug the joiner here!

**Flute**: Francis Flute the bellows mender here!

**Snout**: Snout the tinker here!

**Quince**: Good. I've written a play for the Duke's wedding. It is the sad tale of Pyramus and Thisbe. You, Bottom, will be Pyramus. Flute will be our heroine, Thisbe. We will meet tonight to rehearse in secret deep in the woods.

(*All exit.*)

Adapted from *A Midsummer Night's Dream* by William Shakespeare

**1** Match the summaries below to the character that said them.

Hermia •                    • Let's go to my aunt's.

Lysander •                  • I want Demetrius to love me.

Helena •                    • I don't want to marry Demetrius.

Philostrate •               • Silence please!

**2** *Pyramus, our leading man*

*leading man* is closest in meaning to…

Tick **one**.

the boss.        ☐

the victim.      ☐

the star.        ☐

the criminal.    ☐

**3** This text tells you that Hermia doesn't want to marry Demetrius. Write **two** key details that tell you this.

1. _____

2. _____

**4** Who seems to be in charge of the Mechanicals' play?

Tick **one**.

Starveling   ☐

Quince       ☐

Flute        ☐

Bottom       ☐

**5** What might happen to the characters in this playscript in the woods that night?
Explain, fully, referring to the text in your answer.

_____
_____
_____
_____
_____

# Marlene gives chase

These questions will help you practise:
* ★ making and explaining inferences
* ★ understanding words in context
* ★ summarising main ideas
* ★ making comparisons
* ★ making predictions.

That was the moment the dog came bounding out at us from the trees, barking wildly. I saw at once it was the same Alsatian that had been tormenting Marlene through the gate. Mutti was running at him, clapping her hands and shouting at him, but the dog would not be put off, would not go away. Instead he circled round behind Marlene, snarling and growling at her. That was what made Marlene suddenly whirl around to face him, sending Karli sprawling into the snow. I ran to him at once and helped him to his feet. By the time I looked up again, Marlene was charging off through the snow, chasing the dog away, trumpeting as she went, her trunk flailing, her ears in full sail. And Mutti was stumbling after her, calling for her to stop. But I could see that there would be no stopping Marlene now, until she had either chased the dog out of sight, or had trampled him to death.

I took Karli by the hand and we both followed Mutti, running through the snow after Marlene. But the snow was deep and we soon tired, and were reduced to a walk. Ahead of us the chase went on. However hard the dog tried to bound away over the snow and escape, Marlene kept after him. All the while her trumpeting was echoing through the park, and louder now in my ears than seemed possible – until I began to realise that it was not Marlene's trumpeting I was hearing at all, but the sound of the air-raid sirens wailing over the city. I stopped to listen to be quite sure my ears were not playing tricks on me.

Karli gripped my arm. 'An air raid!' he cried. 'An air raid!' All I knew then was that we had to get to the shelter, fast as we had been taught. Ahead of us, Mutti too had stopped in her tracks. She was yelling out to Marlene to come back. Again and again she called, but Marlene just kept going. She was almost out of sight now in amongst the trees, as Mutti came stumbling back towards us.

'There is nothing more we can do for now, children,' she said. 'We shall find her later. We must get home, to the shelter. Come quickly!' She grabbed Karli's hand. 'No!' Karli cried, pulling away from her and turning to run. 'No! We can't! We can't leave her. We have to catch her! I'm going after her. You go home if you like. I'm not coming.'

*An Elephant in the Garden* by Michael Morpurgo

**1** What or who is *Marlene*?
Refer to the text to support your answer.

_____

_____

**2** Which word tells you how the dog moved through the snow?

_____

**3** What are the animals doing in this story?
Write **one** sentence.

_____

**4** Using evidence from the text, explain how you know that this story is set in the past.

_____

_____

**5** How are Mutti's actions different in the first paragraph compared to the last paragraph?

_____

_____

**6** What do Karli's actions in the final paragraph tell you about his character?
Give **two** things.

1. _____

2. _____

**7** What might happen to Karli?

_____

_____

# The magician's nephew

These questions will help you practise:
* ★ understanding words in context
* ★ identifying how language choices enhance meaning
* ★ identifying key details
* ★ explaining inferences
* ★ identifying how information is related.

First came the hansom. There was no one in the driver's seat. On the roof – not sitting, but standing on the roof – swaying with superb balance as it came at full speed round the corner with one wheel in the air – was Jadis the Queen of Queens and the Terror of Charn. Her teeth were bared, her eyes shone like fire, and her long hair streamed out behind her like a comet's tail. She was flogging the horse without mercy. Its nostrils were wide and red and its sides were spotted with foam. It galloped madly up to the front door, missing the lamp-post by an inch, and then reared up on its hind legs. The hansom crashed into the lamp-post and shattered into several pieces. The Witch, with a magnificent jump, had sprung clear just in time and landed on the horse's back. She settled herself astride and leaned forward, whispering things in its ear. They must have been things meant not to quiet it but to madden it. It was on its hind legs again in a moment, and its neigh was like a scream; it was all hoofs and teeth and eyes and tossing mane. Only a splendid rider could have stayed on its back.

Before Digory had recovered his breath, a good many other things began to happen. A second hansom dashed up close behind the first; out of there jumped a fat man in a frock-coat and a policeman. Then came a third hansom with two more policemen in it. After it came about twenty people (mostly errand boys) on bicycles, all ringing their bells and letting out cheers and cat-calls. Last of all came a crowd of people on foot, all very hot with running, but obviously enjoying themselves. Windows shot up in all the houses of that street and a housemaid or a butler appeared at every front door. They wanted to see the fun.

Meanwhile an old gentleman had begun to struggle shakily out of the ruins of the first hansom. Several people rushed forward to help him; but as one pulled him one way and another another, perhaps he would have got out quite as quickly on his own. Digory guessed that the old gentleman must be Uncle Andrew but you couldn't see his face; his tall hat had been bashed down over it.

C.S. Lewis

**1** What is a *hansom*?

Tick **one**.

a butler ☐

a horse-drawn carriage ☐

a horse ☐

a driver ☐

1

(1 mark)

**2** The sentence beginning *Her teeth were bared* contains two **similes**.

a) **Find** and **copy one** of them.

_____

2a

(1 mark)

b) Explain the effect of the simile you have chosen.

_____

_____

2b

(1 mark)

**3** *The Witch, with a magnificent jump, had sprung clear just in time and landed on the horse's back.*

Underline the group of words that show the Witch was under pressure to land.

3

(1 mark)

**4** The horse was very wild.

Write **two** details from the text that support this statement.

1. _____

2. _____

4

(2 marks)

**5** Do you think the queen was a good rider?

Explain how you know, referring to the text in your answer.

5

(3 marks)

_____

_____

_____

_____

_____

/ 9

Total for
this text

# Stig of the dump

These questions will help you practise:
★ summarising main ideas
★ making inferences
★ explaining how language choices enhance meaning
★ making predictions.

He lay quiet and looked around the cave again. Now that his eyes were used to it he could see further into the dark part of the cave. There was somebody there! Or Something!

Something, or Somebody, had a lot of shaggy black hair and two bright black eyes that were looking very hard at Barney.

'Hallo!' said Barney.
Something said nothing.
'I fell down the cliff,' said Barney.
Somebody grunted.
'My name's Barney.'
Somebody-Something made a noise that sounded like 'Stig'.

'D'you think you could help me undo my feet, Mr Stig?' asked Barney politely. 'I've got a pocket-knife,' he added, remembering that he had in his pocket a knife he'd found among the wood-shavings on the floor of Grandfather's workshop. It was quite a good knife except that one blade had come off and the other one was broken in half and rather blunt.

Good thing I put it in my pocket, he thought. He wriggled so he could reach the knife, and managed to open the rusty half-blade. He tried to reach the creepers round his legs, but found it was difficult to cut creepers with a blunt knife when your feet are tied above your head.

The Thing sitting in the corner seemed to be interested. It got up and moved towards Barney into the light. Barney was glad to see it was Somebody after all. Funny way to dress though, he thought, rabbit-skins round the middle and no shoes or socks.

'Oh puff!' said Barney. 'I can't reach my feet. You do it, Stig!'

He handed the knife to Stig.

Stig turned it over and felt it with his strong hairy hands, and tested the edge with a thumb. Then instead of trying to cut the creepers he squatted down on the ground and picked up a broken stone.

He's going to sharpen the knife, thought Barney.

But no, it seemed more as if he were sharpening the stone. Using the hard knife to chip with, Stig was carefully flaking tiny splinters off the edge of the flint, until he had a thin sharp blade. Then he sprang up, and with two or three slashes cut through the creeper that tied Barney's feet.

Barney sat up. 'Golly!' he said. 'You *are* clever! I bet my Grandad couldn't do that, and he's *very* good at making things.'

Stig grinned. Then he went to the back of the cave and hid the broken knife under a pile of rubbish.

'My knife!' protested Barney. But Stig took no notice. Barney got up and went into the dark part of the cave.

Clive King

**1** What does this text tell you about Stig's skills?

_____

_____

**2** Look at the first paragraph.
How does the writer create tension at the start of the text?
Give **two** ways.

1. _____

2. _____

**3** Why do you think Barney was glad to see it was a _Somebody after all_?

_____

_____

**4** What effect do you think the writer tries to create by writing:

_Something said nothing._

_Somebody grunted._

_Somebody-Something made a noise…?_

Explain your answer fully.

_____

_____

_____

**5** What do you think Barney did next? Use the text to support your answer.

_____

_____

**6** Number the events from **1** to **4** in the order they happen in the text.

Stig hid the knife at the back of the cave. ☐

Barney saw something at the back of the cave. ☐

Stig used the stone to release Barney. ☐

Barney fell into the cave. ☐

# God escapes to the sky

These questions will help you practise:
★ making inferences
★ understanding words in context
★ making comparisons
★ summarising main ideas.

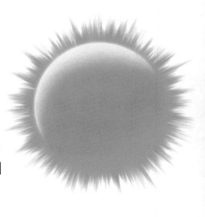

When the earth was first made, Nyambi, the creator, lived happily amongst his creatures with his wife, Nasilele. But Kamonu, the leader of humankind, was cleverer than the rest. He learnt how to sculpt and to forge iron, just like Nyambi. It seemed that whatever Nyambi did, Kamonu wanted to copy.

As time went by, Kamonu grew more ambitious. One day he began to hunt his fellow creatures. This made Nyambi very angry, for he wanted his creatures to live together in peace. 'Stop it!' he cried and banished Kamonu to a far-off land.

Before long, Kamonu returned. Nyambi pardoned him and gave Kamonu a garden where he could grow his own food. But soon Kamonu was up to his old tricks, hunting the buffaloes and antelopes. This time Nyambi would not forgive him. He was so cross he decided to leave Kamonu to fend for himself.

First Nyambi and his family moved to a faraway land, but crafty Kamonu made a raft and sailed across the water to meet him. Next he went to the top of a high mountain, but again Kamonu found him. In desperation, Nyambi told his plight to a fortune-teller. 'Spider is the only person who can help you,' the fortune-teller whispered knowingly. And so it was, for Spider came along and spun a very long thread from Earth to Heaven. Up, up, up Nyambi and his followers climbed, to make their home in the sky.

Down below, Kamonu was vexed. Straight away he began to build a log tower that would reach the sky. Higher and higher it grew, until CRASH! it gave way under the weight of the logs. And that was the end of Kamonu's attempt to reach Nyambi. Now Kamonu and his people could only greet their creator as the sun in the morning, and his wife as the moon in the evening.

Annabel Shilson-Thomas

**1** Number the events from **1** to **5** in the order they happen in the text.

The creator moved away to a faraway land. ☐

Nyambi allowed Kamonu to return. ☐

Nyambi sought advice from a fortune-teller. ☐

Kamonu was unable to reach Nyambi. ☐

The creator and leader of humans lived in harmony. ☐

1

(1 mark)

**2** What did Kamonu sail across the water on?

_____

2

(1 mark)

**3** *As time went by, Kamonu grew more ambitious.*

What does the word *ambitious* show you about Kamonu?

Tick **one**.

He wanted all the creatures to live in peace. ☐

He was growing more and more angry with Nyambi. ☐

He wanted to be more powerful than other creatures. ☐

He was more clever than Nyambi and Nasilele. ☐

3

(1 mark)

**4** Write **one** thing that is different about Nyambi's character compared to Kamonu's.

_____

4

(1 mark)

**5** This myth explains one idea about…

Tick **one**.

how god became the sun. ☐

how god left the earth. ☐

how the universe was created. ☐

how humans are destroyers. ☐

5

(1 mark)

**6** At the end of the myth Kamonu is left on earth.
What does the story tell us is the only way he can greet Nyambi and Nasilele now?

Nyambi: _____

Nasilele: _____

6

(2 marks)

/7

Total for
this text

# Beamish, living museum of the North

These questions will help you practise:
★ retrieving and recording information
★ explaining how language choices enhance meaning
★ explaining inferences
★ giving the meaning of words in context
★ making inferences.

Beamish Museum is a world-famous open air museum. It tells the story of life in North East England during the 1820s, 1900s and 1940s.

Beamish stands in 300 acres of beautiful County Durham countryside. With so many things to see, Beamish is a wonderful day out for people of all ages.

## The Town
The Town represents a typical North Eastern market town in the years leading up to the First World War.

## Railway Station
Rowley Station, adjacent to The Town, is a typical country station as it would have been in Edwardian times.

## 1940s Farm
This describes the story of life on the Home Front in the rural North East and how farming saved the nation from starvation during the war.

## The Colliery
No recreation of the history of North East England would be complete without a **colliery** and the people who worked and lived around it.

See how **pit** communities were in the early 1900s. Villages grew up around the mines, houses and coal were provided free in exchange for **labour**.

## Pockerley Waggonway
This operating railway gives a flavour of rail travel in the early 1800s as it cuts through the Georgian landscape in the valley below Pockerley Old Hall.

Most of the houses, shops and other buildings you see here have been brought to Beamish, rebuilt and furnished as they once were. Some, such as Home Farm, Pockerley Old Hall and the drift mine, were here already.

You won't find objects displayed in glass cases at Beamish, you'll see them in their original context. What's more, you will meet our costumed staff who are proud of their **heritage** and happy to share their knowledge with visitors.

If you don't fancy walking, there are vintage trams and buses, including our Access bus, to make travelling around the museum easier, and even more exciting!

## Glossary
- **colliery** a coal mine and all the buildings and machines connected with it
- **pit** coal mine
- **labour** practical effort and hard work
- **heritage** features belonging to a particular culture or society, such as buildings which were created in the past and are still historically important

1   According to the text, if you don't fancy walking, how else can you travel around the museum?
    Give **two** ways.

    1.  _____

    2.  _____

2   Which place do you need to visit to find information on food during the war?

    _____

3   What is the effect of describing the Beamish museum staff in the text?

    _____

    _____

4   Explain why this might be an interesting place to visit for those who are interested in history.

    _____

    _____

5   *This operating railway gives a flavour of rail travel in the early 1800s...*

    What does the word *flavour* mean in this phrase?

    _____

6   Using information from the text, tick one box in each row to show whether each statement is a **fact** or an **opinion**.

| | Fact | Opinion |
|---|---|---|
| Beamish is in the North East. | | |
| County Durham has beautiful countryside. | | |
| Beamish is a wonderful day out. | | |
| Houses and coal were free for miners. | | |
| The railway travels through the valley. | | |

# Insects on summer staycation!

These questions will help you practise:
* ★ explaining the meaning of words in context
* ★ retrieving information
* ★ explaining how language choices enhance meaning
* ★ making comparisons
* ★ explaining inferences.

## Do you remember the long, warm, hazy summer of 2014?

Children, gardeners, festival goers and holiday makers all relished, for what seemed an eternity, the wonderful warm weather of summer 2014. It was a huge change to the previous winter of 2013, when torrential downpours and lower temperatures prevailed and continued long into the following spring.

But humans weren't the only ones who benefited from the hot, lazy holiday seasons. Many insects thrived and flourished in what experts have described as a 'crazy, hot and humid heatwave' which forms part of the ever-changing climate in the UK. Scientists explained that these insects flourish in warm, damp conditions, as they provide perfect breeding grounds for laying eggs.

Gardeners saw increases in the numbers of snails and slugs, grazing greedily on their plants. Holiday makers, including campers, suffered with mosquito and horsefly bites during early morning rising and early evening outdoor barbecues.

However, the damp winter weather and warm humid summer created confusion for the life cycle of wasps, and meant that there were fewer than usual – definitely a bonus for seasonal campers.

After studying the data, Dr Eve Philips, an expert in the life cycles of insects joked, 'It's a bit like the perfect summer holiday for biting insects! They have stayed at home and reaped the benefits – an insect staycation!'

Jen Palmer-Jones, from a local bird watching society, was also rejoicing.

'Many species of sea birds including gannets and gulls have prospered due to the change in climate, and possibly because of the increase in insect numbers, as one source of their food.'

**1** *Many insects thrived and flourished...*
What does the word *thrived* tell you about the insects?

_____

**2** The text is telling us that the weather in 2014 was generally...

Tick **one**.

windy and cold.          ☐

dry and hot.             ☐

warm and humid.          ☐

wet and stormy.          ☐

**3** **Find** and **copy one** example of alliteration in the paragraph beginning *Gardeners saw increases...*.
Explain why it has been used.

Example      _____

Explanation  _____

_____

**4** How did the weather make the lives of the common wasps different compared to the lives of seabirds?

_____

_____

**5** The weather in 2014 had both good and bad effects.
Explain fully what these effects were, referring to the text in your answer.

_____
_____
_____
_____
_____

# Tales of childhood

These questions will help you practise:
★ explaining the meaning of words in context
★ retrieving and recording information
★ making inferences
★ making predictions.

After school was over, the same four boys and I would set out together across the village green and through the village itself, heading for home. On the way to school and on the way back we always passed the sweet-shop. No we didn't, we never passed it. We always stopped. We lingered outside its rather small window gazing in at the big glass jars full of Bull's-eyes and Old Fashioned Humbugs and Strawberry Bonbons and Glacier Mints and Acid Drops and Pear Drops and Lemon Drops and all the rest of them. Each of us received sixpence a week for pocket-money, and whenever there was any money in our pockets, we would all troop in together to buy a pennyworth of this or that. My own favourites were Sherbet Suckers and Liquorice Bootlaces.

One of the other boys, whose name was Thwaites, told me I should never eat Liquorice Bootlaces. Thwaites's father, who was a doctor, had said that they were made from rats' blood. The father had given his young son a lecture about Liquorice Bootlaces when he had caught him eating one in bed. 'Every ratcatcher in the country,' the father had said, 'takes his rats to the Liquorice Bootlace Factory, and the manager pays tuppence for each rat. Many a ratcatcher has become a millionaire by selling his dead rats to the Factory.'

'But how do they turn the rats into liquorice?' the young Thwaites had asked his father.

'They wait until they've got ten thousand rats,' the father had answered, 'then they dump them all into a huge shiny steel cauldron and boil them up for several hours. Two men stir the bubbling cauldron with long poles and in the end they have a thick steaming rat-stew. After that, a cruncher is lowered into the cauldron to crunch the bones, and what's left is a pulpy substance called rat-mash.'

'Yes, but how do they turn that into Liquorice Bootlaces, Daddy?' the young Thwaites had asked, and this question, according to Thwaites, had caused his father to pause and think for a few moments before he answered it. At last he had said, 'The two men who were doing the stirring with the long poles now put on their wellington boots and climb into the cauldron and shovel the hot rat-mash out on to a concrete floor. Then they run a steam-roller over it several times to flatten it out. What is left looks rather like a gigantic black pancake, and all they have to do after that is wait for it to cool and to harden so they can cut it up into strips to make the Bootlaces. Don't ever eat them,' the father had said. 'If you do, you'll get ratitis.'

From *Boy – Tales of Childhood* by Roald Dahl

**1** Look at the second paragraph.
What does the word *lecture* tell you about the talk that Thwaites's father had with him?

_____

_____

1
(1 mark)

**2** Circle the correct option to complete the sentence below.

When the boys passed the sweet-shop they…

| went in. | | bought sweets. | | passed it. | | stopped. |
|---|---|---|---|---|---|---|

2
(1 mark)

**3** In the final paragraph, why did Thwaites's father have to pause and think before he explained how to turn the rat-mash into bootlaces?

_____

_____

3
(1 mark)

**4** Do you think Thwaites will eat Liquorice Bootlaces again? Explain why, referring to the text in your answer.

_____

_____

_____

_____

_____

4
(3 marks)

**5** **Find** and **copy two** examples from the text which show how important and exciting the sweet-shop was to the boys.

_____

_____

_____

5
(2 marks)

/ 8

Total for
this text

# The Earth's layers

These questions will help you practise:
★ identifying how information in non-fiction is related
★ retrieving and recording information
★ identifying language choices
★ explaining how information in non-fiction contributes to meaning
★ making inferences
★ summarising main ideas.

## Understanding Earth Science

### Atmosphere

● The atmosphere is made up of gases surrounding the Earth. The different layers have different temperatures.

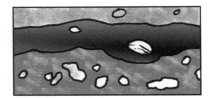

### Lithosphere

● The lithosphere is made up of rocky materials in the crust and upper mantle. It includes the land beneath the continents and oceans.

### Hydrosphere

● The hydrosphere is the zone made up of all the water on Earth (the word 'hydro' means water). It includes not only the large oceans and seas, but also the smaller lakes, rivers, ponds and streams that make up two thirds of the Earth's surface.

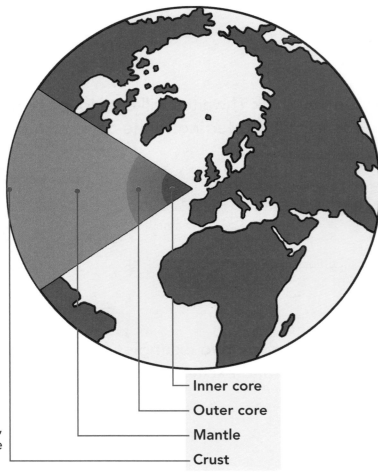

Inner core
Outer core
Mantle
Crust

### Biosphere

● The biosphere overlaps the other three spheres. It is where living things can exist. Life can be found in the water, deep inside the Earth and high up in the atmosphere.

# Answers and mark scheme

**Pigeon summer (pages 6–7)**
1  2a – 1 mark – *staring*
2  2g – 1 mark – *blasted*
3  2c – 1 mark for all four correctly ordered:
Mary hung the washing by the fire. *3*
Mary went outside to shut the pigeons away. *4*
Mary's mum did the ironing. *2*
Mary's mum thrust the washing basket at Mary. *1*
4  2h – 1 mark. Both characters must be referenced in the answer. Mary is watching the pigeons but Phyl is helping Mum/putting Lennie to bed.
5  2b – 2 marks. 1 mark for each answer from the following: '*Get the washing in, for heaven's sake!*' snapped Mum./'*Standing there gawping up at those birds. You never think.*'/She thrust the basket at Mary./She went in, slamming the door, leaving Mary outside./She repeats, '*You never think*' a second time.
6  2e – 2 marks for an action with a reason. Possible answers: She will go after Mary and make her take the ironing upstairs, the last thing she asked her to do./She will get Mary and send her to her room for being cheeky/disrespectful./She needs time to calm down so will leave Mary alone and take the ironing up herself./She knows Mary is upset about the pigeon so she will leave her outside to calm down.
1 mark for an action. Possible answers: Go after Mary./Send her to her room./Do the ironing./Leave her alone.

**The wind in the willows (pages 8–9)**
1  2b – 1 mark – *revitalised*.
2  2b – 2 marks. 1 mark for each answer from the following: He threw his brush on the floor and said, '*Hang spring-cleaning!*'/He scrabbled to the drive leading to where the animals lived *nearer to the sun and air*./When he popped up in the meadow, he said, '*This is better than whitewashing!*'
3  2a – 1 mark. It is suitable because it explains the movement of spring through Mole's house./Filtering through; penetrating; entering every room.
4  2b – 1 mark. …*residences are nearer to the sun and air*.
5  2b/2g – 1 mark. *Scraped, scratched, scrabbled, scrooged*; *divine discontent*.
6  2d – Award 3 marks for fully developed response with reference to the text: It is very dirty and dusty. He hasn't looked after it. Mole had dust in his throat and eyes and his back and arms ached from so much cleaning which tells you that it hadn't been cleaned for a long time.
Award 2 marks for fully developed response: It is very dirty and dusty. Mole had dust in his throat and eyes.
Award 1 mark for undeveloped response: It was dusty and dirty.

**A sudden puff of glittering smoke (pages 10–11)**
1  a) 2b – 1 mark – *rings around a planet*
   b) 2b – 1 mark. The writer uses a simile – *like rings around a planet*. It creates an image of how the mist swirled around Jeanie, in the same way as rings circle a planet, something which may be more familiar to the reader.
2  2f – 1 mark – *In the good old days*
3  2b – 2 marks. 1 mark each for two of the following: *The genie shut his eyes till his dark lashes fluttered on his cheeks./He blew and blew./But the genie still blew./The glittering rings still circled round her head*.
4  2a – 1 mark. To throw the heat back: white-wash reflects heat so it is like saying it threw/bounced/reflected it straight back.

5  2d – 2 marks for developed answer: Mr Piper's eyes widened and his mouth dropped open which means he could not believe what he was hearing./He said to Jeanie that he thought she *must have spent the whole weekend locked in the library, to know so much*./He may not have thought that Jeanie was capable of knowing such information as this. 1 mark for undeveloped points such as: His mouth dropped./He didn't think Jeannie knew much./He thought she'd been to the library.

**A Tudor girl's diary (pages 12–13)**
1  2b – 1 mark. The swordsman was delayed on the road./Something had happened on the road so the swordsman couldn't make it on time.
2  2b – Award 1 mark for all four correct: true/false/false/true
3  2d – 1 mark. To protect them from the horror of the execution./To keep them away from the execution which would be a terrible thing for children to see.
4  2d – 2 marks. 1 mark each for two answers referring to Henry's behaviour: Henry had lots of parties and celebrations with music and feasting./*Henry has been behaving with a gaiety that most of us find distasteful*.
5  2d – 2 marks. She did not like/support Anne Boleyn as she called her '*that woman*' and insisted on seeing her executed '*for the sake of Queen Catherine*'.
6  2c – 1 mark. Answers relating to the beheading of the queen in newspaper language, e.g. The Day The Queen Died/The Execution of Anne/The Queen Protests Her Innocence.

**A midsummer night's dream (pages 14–15)**
1  2b – 2 marks.

| | |
|---|---|
| Hermia | I don't want to marry Demetrius. |
| Lysander | Let's go to my aunt's. |
| Helena | I want Demetrius to love me. |
| Philostrate | Silence please! |

2  2a – 1 mark – *the star*.
3  2b – 2 marks. Award 1 mark each for two of the following: She tells Lysander that she loves him./*It is you who I love*./She is going to run away with Lysander to marry him./She is going to meet Lysander at the gate to run away with him.
4  2d – 1 mark – *Quince*
5  2e – 3 marks. Accept answers relating to the rehearsal and characters in the woods: As the Mechanicals rehearse, the lovers find them and their secret is revealed./As the Mechanicals rehearse, they overhear the lovers in the woods and go to tell the Duke and Egeus.

**Marlene gives chase (pages 16–17)**
1  2d – *she went, her trunk flailing, her ears in full sail* and that's what elephants do.
2  2a – 1 mark – *bounding*
3  2c – 1 mark. An elephant has run off into the trees to chase a dog./An elephant, after chasing a dog, is lost in the trees during an air raid.
4  2d – 1 mark. There was an air-raid siren./They had to get to the (air-raid) shelter.
5  2h – 1 mark for comparison in both the first and last paragraphs.
In the first paragraph, Mutti runs after the elephant to try to bring it back. In the last paragraph, she gives up running because she knows it's important to return to the shelter.
In the first paragraph, Mutti was running after the elephant calling for her to stop. In the last paragraph,

Mutti stopped chasing the elephant to return to the shelter.

6 2d – 2 marks. 1 mark for one of the following linked to caring for the animal: loving; thoughtful; concerned; worried. Any one of the following linked to taking a risk: brave; silly; disrespectful; dangerous.

7 2e – 1 mark for answers relating to past events in the story. He might get hurt in the bombing raid as the air-raid sirens mean that there is bombing to come. / He might get bitten by the Alsatian who is being followed by Marlene. / He might get lost and cold in the trees in the snow and never be able to find his way out. / He might find Marlene, calm her down and make his way back to his family.

## The magician's nephew (pages 18–19)

1 2a – 1 mark – *a horse-drawn carriage*

2 a) 2b – 1 mark – *Eyes shone like fire; Long hair streamed out behind her like a comet's tail.*
   b) 2g – 1 mark. The writer wants the reader to visualise the intense sparkling colour of her eyes in the same way as the colourful flames of a fire sparkle and shine. The writer wants to give the reader the effect of movement of her hair flowing behind her in the same way as a comet's tail.

3 2f – 1 mark – *just in time*

4 2b – 2 marks. 1 mark each for two of the following: Its nostrils were wide and red. / Its sides were covered in foam. / It galloped madly. / It reared up on its hind legs. / Its neigh was like a scream.

5 2d – Award 3 marks for two reasons with reference to the text.
   Award 2 marks for one reason with text evidence or two reasons without evidence.
   Award 1 mark for one reason without evidence.
   Standing on the roof as the carriage moved at high speed which means she has good balance and control. / Superb balance on the moving carriage. / She jumped from the carriage as it crashed and onto the horse's back. / She stood on the roof. / She jumped onto the horse's back.

## Stig of the dump (pages 20–21)

1 2d – 1 mark. Answer relating to using the knife: He is very good at using tools / the knife.

2 2g – 2 marks. 1 mark each for two of the following: Withholds information; refers to the character as 'he' and doesn't give his name; tells that the character is in a dark cave; writes two short sentences ending with exclamation marks; doesn't tell the reader who or what is with him in the dark cave.

3 2d – 1 mark. The 'something' might have been a dangerous / scary animal. He can talk to a person and ask for help.

4 2g – 2 marks for developed explanation: To create a mysterious / strange / baffling mood by withholding the identity of the something or somebody. / The writer uses short sentences which create suspense or mystery.
   Award 1 mark for undeveloped points: To make it sound strange. / For mystery.

5 2e – 1 mark for answers relating to past events in the text such as the taking of the knife: Barney took the knife from where Stig had just hidden it and told Stig it wasn't his. / Barney looked around in the back of the cave for his knife. / Barney stood at the back of the cave and told Stig he wouldn't leave until his knife was returned.

6 2c – 1 mark for all four correctly ordered:
   Stig hid the knife at the back of the cave. *4*
   Barney saw something at the back of the cave. *2*
   Stig used the stone to release Barney. *3*
   Barney fell into the cave. *1*

## God escapes to the sky (pages 22–23)

1 2c – 1 mark for all five text boxes correctly ordered:
   The creator moved away to a faraway land. *3*
   Nyambi allowed Kamonu to return. *2*
   Nyambi sought advice from a fortune-teller. *4*
   Kamonu was unable to reach Nyambi. *5*
   The creator and leader of humans lived in harmony. *1*

2 2b – 1 mark. A raft.

3 2a – 1 mark – *He wanted to be more powerful than other creatures.*

4 2h – 1 mark for one of the following: Nyambi wanted creatures to live in peace / Kamonu wanted to hunt creatures; Kamonu was ambitious / Nyambi was not; Nyambi wanted to live away from Kamonu / Kamonu wanted to live near to Nyambi.

5 2c – 1 mark – *how god left the earth.*

6 2b – 2 marks. 1 mark for each: *Nyambi*: as the sun in the morning. *Nasilele*: as the moon in the evening.

## Beamish, living museum of the North (pages 24–25)

1 2b – 2 marks. Any two of the following: vintage trams / buses / Access bus.

2 2b – 1 mark – 1940s farm

3 2g – 1 mark. To encourage / persuade the reader to visit the museum. / To encourage the reader to find out about the history / knowledge of the museum. / To encourage the reader's curiosity about local history. / To tell the reader that they can find out information about local history from the people who work there.

4 2b – 1 mark. It gives you a good idea of what life was like for people living and working from the 1800s. / It has real working examples of what life would have looked like in the 1800s onwards. / It gives historians first-hand evidence of life in Durham from the 1800s onwards.

5 2a – 1 mark – idea / impression / suggestion

6 2d – 1 mark for three or four correct and 2 marks for all five correct: fact / opinion / opinion / fact / fact

## Insects on summer staycation! (pages 26–27)

1 2a – 1 mark – They were healthy / increasing in numbers.

2 2b – 1 mark – *warm and humid.*

3 2g – 2 marks. 1 mark for alliteration: grazing greedily. 1 mark for effect: To give the effect of gluttonous or continuous eating habits of the slugs and snails.

4 2h – 1 mark. The wasps struggled / could not breed / there weren't many of them, compared to seabirds who had good breeding seasons.

5 2d – Award 3 marks for fully developed response for both outcomes: The warm weather meant that it was good for creepy crawlies and other insects which could breed for longer and have a longer life. This is not good for people who don't like them, especially mosquitoes which can transmit infections. The weather wasn't good for gardeners or farmers because there were lots of snails and slugs around to eat the plants.
   Award 2 marks for fully developed response for one outcome: The warm weather meant that it was good for creepy crawlies and other insects which could breed for longer and have a longer life.
   Award 1 mark for undeveloped point.
   The weather wasn't good for wasps as there were so few.

## Tales of childhood (pages 28–29)

1 2a – 1 mark. To give an educational talk about the dangers of eating bootlaces. / To warn him of the dangers of eating bootlaces by giving him the facts.

2 2b – 1 mark. *stopped.*

3 2d – 1 mark. He couldn't think how the rest of the story would go. / He didn't have any other ideas to make up about the end of the story. / He had run out of ideas. / He couldn't think of any more lies to tell.

4 2e – Award 3 marks for fully developed answers referring to the text: No. His father has given him a disgusting explanation of how they are made, using *rats* caught by *ratcatchers*. Also, his father has warned him that if he does, he will get *ratitis*.
Yes. I don't think the boy believes his father at all. Rats have nothing to do with liquorice. The story about catching the rats, crunching the bones and steam-rollering them is unbelievable. The boy might love the bootlaces anyway, so it wouldn't matter how they are made.
Award 2 marks for fully developed answers:
Yes. I don't think the boy believes his father at all. Rats have nothing to do with liquorice.
No. His father has given him a disgusting explanation of how they are made, using rats caught by *ratcatchers*.
Award 1 mark for undeveloped point: No. He might get ill.

5 2f – 2 marks. 1 mark for each correct example from the text, e.g. *We never passed it. We always stopped.* / *whenever there was any money in our pockets we would all troop in* / *We lingered outside... gazing in at the big jars.*

### The Earth's layers (pages 30–31)

1 2c – 1 mark – Award 1 mark for an alternative heading which successfully summarises the contents of the poster, e.g. *Understanding the Earth's Layers*, *What are the Earth's Layers?*

2 2f – 1 mark – *to inform*

3 2b – 1 mark – the biosphere

4 2b – 2 marks. 1 mark each for two words such as: *atmosphere, lithosphere, hydrosphere, biosphere.*

5 2f – 1 mark for any of the following: To show the reader what the layers of the Earth look like as there is no written information on this. / To show where the Earth's spheres are. / The diagram helps the reader to understand the written information on each sphere. / The diagram shows the reader the position of the spheres around the Earth.

6 2d – 1 mark – a scientist; someone interested in the Earth; a geologist; someone studying science or geography

### Colour your autumn (pages 32–33)

1 2b / 2g – 1 mark – three possible answers: *light hits the earth at a different angle*; *long, low sunbeams*; *golden glow.*

2 2b – 1 mark for any of the following: Inspired by Sleeping Beauty (retold by Charles Perrault). / There was once a structure called the Sleeping Parlour.

3 2f – 1 mark – *cause and effect*

4 2d – 2 marks for link between subject and text. Science / Physics. It talks about the scientific effect of the tilting of the earth in autumn and how the sunlight hits the earth at a different angle.
1 mark for subject: Science / Physics

5 2g – 1 mark. To give the image of a very impressive range of colours. / To suggest a range of random and varied colours.

6 2g – 2 marks for developed answer with reference to sight and taste (feeling could be included). References to the text are included: It refers to examples that relate to your sight by saying which flowers and colours can be seen: a riot of colour to *stimulate your eyes* / *produce to delight your eyes.* / It relates to your feelings: *to warm your heart.* / To taste – produce to *whet your appetite.*
1 mark for undeveloped points referring to one or more of the senses: sight / taste; sight for colours; taste for food from gardens or in the café.

### ZSL Whipsnade Zoo (pages 34–35)

1 2f – 2 marks. 1 mark each for the following: To break the text into chunks that are easier to read. / It's easier to find the section you want.

2 2f – 1 mark – *to persuade and inform*

3 2b – 2 marks. 1 mark each for two of the following: *fantastic; amazing; delicious; don't miss; unique chance; see more than ever before.*

4 2d – 1 mark – It is delicious.

5 2b – 2 marks. 1 mark each for two of the following: It is nine foot high. / You can see a view of the entire paddock. / It provides a view of the indoor barn on cold days.

### Jacqueline Wilson at Christmas (pages 36–37)

1 2b – 1 mark – America

2 2b – 2 marks. 1 mark each for two of the following: The writer loves things to do with Christmas. / The writer has a favourite Christmas movie; children's Christmas book; Christmas song; Christmas theatre show; Christmas TV show; Christmas painting.

3 2c – 1 mark for all correct:
Film        takes the writer into a wonderful world
Book        starts sad but ends happily
Television  full of heart-warming stories
Music       a very familiar festive version

4 2g – 1 mark – It is energetic, lively, determined, etc.

5 2f – 1 mark – blog. The writer uses the first person pronoun / words such as *my, I.* / It is written in the present tense. / It provides details / facts / events of the writer's life.

6 2d – 2 marks. Award 1 mark each for any two opinions, e.g. *I don't think anything beats the moment when …*; *sing medieval songs very beautifully*; *is very truthful*; *is just a lovely picture.*

### The orang-utan nursery (pages 38–39)

1 2d – 1 mark for three or four correct and 2 marks for all five correct: fact / opinion / fact / fact / opinion

2 2c – 1 mark – *Bulu Mata needs a new mother.*

3 2a – 1 mark – *caring.*

4 2b – 2 marks. 1 mark each for the following: Sudocrem; Bonjela.

5 2e – 2 marks. Award 2 marks for developed answers related to the adoption: Hsaio-qua will adopt him because she has adopted another before and the staff think she is ready for another challenge. / Hsaio-qua will not adopt him and he won't have a mother. It says that she is yet to pick him up, like she did with the other baby she adopted.
Award 1 mark for undeveloped points: She will adopt him. / She won't adopt him.

### The history of chocolate (pages 40–41)

1 2b – 1 mark – Sweeten it.

2 2d – 1 mark for all four correctly ticked: opinion / fact / fact / opinion

3 2f – 1 mark. It is effective because it has been ordered chronologically / in order of time.
There is a short paragraph of information for each time period.
Information can be read in any order according to the period of time.

4 2c – 1 mark. *Chocolate has been popular for centuries.*

5 2d – Award 2 marks for responses referring to the text: Perhaps it wasn't sweet enough. The text says that it became more popular when the Spanish began to sweeten the drink.
Award 1 mark for undeveloped point: It wasn't sweet. / It was bitter / sour.

### The 'walk to school' debate (pages 42–43)

1 2c – 1 mark – *to discuss*

2 2d – 1 mark for all four correct responses: fact / fact / opinion / opinion

3 2e – 1 mark. There could be an increase in the amount of air pollution.

4 2b – 2 marks. 1 mark each for two of the following: It is more healthy for you. / It aids physical wellbeing. / It makes you more aware. / You daydream less. / You improve socially in school. / Children become more independent. / The roads would be safer and cleaner.

5 2h – 2 marks. 1 mark each for two of the following: Children are safer. / Parents don't have to rush to get to work. / Children are supervised. / Short car trips don't cause much pollution.

## The sound collector (pages 44–45)

1 2g – 1 mark – *onomatopoeia*

2 2a – 1 mark. Answers related to the sound or the beat of a drum: It tells the reader how the sound of the rain is similar to the sound of a drum. / It is a metaphor comparing the rhythm of the rain to the beat of a drum.

3 2b – 1 mark – *The bubbling of the bathtub*

4 2g – 1 mark. The effect is to give the poem a kind of 'sing song' rhythm which makes it predictable and easier to read.

5 2f – 1 mark – *A stranger called this morning*

6 2d – 1 mark. There will be no sound in the house. / The house will be silent when, usually, it is very noisy.

## The reader of this poem (pages 46–47)

1 2g – 1 mark. To make the reader repeat the words as they read in the same way as an echo repeats.

2 2f – 1 mark. To shock / scare / surprise the reader in the way a ghost would. / To change the reader's voice to a shout, as they might if they saw a ghost.

3 2b – 1 mark for all answers correct: cracked as a cup, brash as a brush, bossy as a whistle, hungry as a wave.

4 a) 2b – 1 mark for any simile.
   b) 2g – 1 mark for explaining the effect of the comparison in the simile chosen in 4a.

5 2d – Award 3 marks for fully developed response with reference to the text: To tell the reader that the insults weren't meant. The poem contains a list of insults about the reader's character, such as *As troublesome as bubblegum*; *As sneaky as a witch's spell*; *As bossy as a whistle*; *As vain as trainers*. The reader could take this the wrong way, but the writer doesn't really want the reader to feel insulted, but to take the descriptions in a light-hearted way, like a joke.
Award 2 marks for fully developed response: The writer wants the reader to know the poem is really a joke, because it contains a list of insults about the reader's character, such as *As troublesome as bubblegum*; *As sneaky as a witch's spell*; *As bossy as a whistle*; *As vain as trainers*.
Award 1 mark for undeveloped points: The poem is full of insults. / The writer doesn't want the reader to feel upset / insulted.

## Pumpkin for Maxine (pages 48–49)

1 2b – 1 mark for a correctly found and copied example of personification: *Ouch, it said, this is worse than the dentist*. / *Pumpkin complained*.

2 2g – 1 mark. To differentiate between the speech of the humans and that of the pumpkin. / To show when the pumpkin speaks.

3 2a – 1 mark. *Oblivious* describes how Mum is unaware of the pain she is causing to the pumpkin. She continues to hurt the pumpkin by emptying the contents of its head.

4 2b – 2 marks. 1 mark each for two of the following: The pumpkin said, 'Ouch, this is worse than the dentist'. / 'Ouch, my cheekbone'. / 'I've got a dreadful headache.'

5 2d – Award 3 marks for fully developed response with reference to the text: The writer felt *frightened* at first when the pumpkin first spoke. When Mum asked the

child to '*dig in*' the child started feeling *dizzy, giddy, all out of sorts* which means s/he didn't like what was happening to it.
Award 2 marks for developed response: Frightened when it spoke. *Dizzy, giddy, all out of sorts* means s/he was worried.
Award 1 mark for undeveloped points: *dizzy, giddy, all out of sorts*.

## Me and my brother (pages 50–51)

1 2f – 1 mark – *as a conversation*

2 2f – 1 mark. By showing how the children are annoying / being rude / disrespectful to their dad by saying things behind his back and repeating phrases he says.

3 2g – 1 mark. To show that dad is angry and is shouting.

4 2d – 1 mark for explaining that his brother was imitating his dad behind his dad's back and that it was funny.

5 2c – 1 mark – rudeness / disrespect / naughtiness.

6 2e – 2 marks. 1 mark each for two of the following: He might say, *Never let me see you doing that again*. / *It's no laughing matter*. / *Now you are in really big trouble*.

7 2b – 1 mark – *good at imitating people*.

## Silver (pages 52–53)

1 2b – 1 mark for a correctly found and copied example of personification in the poem, e.g. *she peers / her beams*.

2 2g – 1 mark – To give the effect of the moon giving a silver colour to the objects below. / To show that they are silver in colour from the moon's light.

3 2a – 1 mark – A house / home / perch for birds.

4 2f / 2g – Award 3 marks for fully developed response with reference to the text: By including description of animals that are asleep and are not moving, such as the dog sleeps in his kennel *like a log*; the doves are asleep in their cote; the fish are *moveless* in the stream.
Award 2 marks for developed answer: By saying the dog, the doves and the fish are asleep and not moving.
Award 1 mark for undeveloped point: The animals are asleep.

5 2c – 1 mark – At night, the moon quietly moves and shines on all objects below.

## The centipede's song (pages 54–55)

1 2b – Award 1 mark for all four correct.

| | |
|---|---|
| mice | rice |
| minced doodlebugs | curried slugs |
| scrambled dregs | hornets stewed in tar |
| snails | lizards' tails |

2 2f – 1 mark – To give additional information / further imagery about the type of food in the verse. / To give the reader further instructions or detail about the food in the verse.

3 2f / 2g – 2 marks. 1 mark each for the following: By using nonsense words such as *dandyprats* and *slobbages*. / By including foods that the centipede thinks are delicious, but are actually disgusting, such as jellied gnats and lizards' tails.

4 2c – 1 mark for any of the following: Strange creatures are delicious to eat. / The reader should try eating the creatures as they are nice to eat. / The narrator has eaten many different / strange / delicious creatures.

5 2d – Award 3 marks for a developed answer referring to the text: The narrator would enjoy eating other revolting things such as minibeasts and creatures that people would not usually choose like spiders and woodlice, rotten eggs and decaying plants. He says, *I've eaten fresh mudburgers by the greatest cooks there are* which proves he likes disgusting food.
Award 2 marks for a developed answer: He would enjoy eating rotten and stinking things like decaying plants.
Award 1 mark for an undeveloped answer: Something rotten; other minibeasts.

**1** Write an alternative heading for the poster.

_____

1 (1 mark)

**2** What is the purpose of this poster?

Tick **one**.

to persuade ☐

to instruct ☐

to entertain ☐

to inform ☐

2 (1 mark)

**3** In which zone would you find living creatures and plants?

_____

3 (1 mark)

**4** Scientific vocabulary is used in this text.
**Find** and **copy two** examples.

1. _____

2. _____

4 (2 marks)

**5** Explain why the writer has included a **diagram** in this poster.

_____

_____

5 (1 mark)

**6** Who might be interested in a poster like this?

_____

6 (1 mark)

/ 7

Total for
this text

# Colour your autumn

It's not your imagination, the light really is different at this time of year. The earth tilts as it orbits the sun so the light hits the earth at a different angle, creating long, low sunbeams and the golden glow that makes this gilded season unique.

There is a richness about the colours of autumn which we hope you will enjoy with us this year in our houses, gardens and countryside.

As memories of summer fade, and the days of early autumn feel a little chillier, there is a riot of colour inside our historic houses waiting to warm your heart and stimulate your eyes.

These richly colourful interiors were often inspired by the colours of nature in the surrounding gardens, parkland and countryside which take on a rich, mellow glow at this time of year.

Many gardens enjoy a renewed blast of colour in autumn with dazzling dahlias and cheery chrysanthemums, and kitchen gardens are positively bursting with produce to delight your eyes and whet your appetite.

## Golden landscapes

Do you often fancy a walk but can't think where to go? There are lots of walks on our website to help you enjoy the best of our autumn colour, from woodland tapestries of yellow, orange, gold and amber, to explosions of rich russet and fluorescent yellows and reds.

## Gorgeous gardens

Many of our gardens have a surprise in store in autumn as the dazzling colour of high summer gives way to the richer hues of late summer blooms such as dahlias and Michaelmas daisies. Harvest time in our walled gardens is also a perfect prompt for a seasonal treat in a tea-room or café where we use home-grown produce wherever we can.

## Colourful stories

All our special places are home to a host of colourful stories from the past, and nowhere more so than Stowe, the magnificent landscape gardens created as a statement of wealth and power in the 18th century, where picturesque paths, temples and monuments are full of hidden meaning and references to the ancient world.

This autumn you can see the recently restored Sleeping Wood, said to have been inspired by the tale of Sleeping Beauty, retold and made popular by Charles Perrault in 1697. There was once a structure called the Sleeping Parlour in the wood, where it's easy to imagine Sleeping Beauty might have lain …

**1**  **Find** and **copy one** phrase from the first paragraph that describes what sunlight is like in autumn.

_____

(1 mark)

**2**  According to the text, how did Sleeping Wood get its name?

_____

(1 mark)

**3**  In the first paragraph, the text is organised in which of the following ways?

(1 mark)

Tick **one**.

cause and effect            ☐

in a sequence               ☐

chronological order         ☐

compare and contrast        ☐

**4**  Which school subject could be taught using the first paragraph? Support your answer using **two** key details from the text.

_____

_____

_____

(2 marks)

**5**  Look at the third paragraph.
Why has the word _riot_ been used to describe the colour inside the houses?

_____

_____

(1 mark)

**6**  How does the writing appeal to the senses?
Refer to the text in your answer.

_____

_____

(2 marks)

/ 8

Total for
this text

# ZSL Whipsnade Zoo

These questions will help you practise:
- ★ explaining how information is related
- ★ identifying how information contributes to meaning
- ★ making inferences
- ★ retrieving and recording information.

Set in over 600 acres, the Zoo is home to over 2,500 animals. From the furry and feathered to the jumbo and majestic, get the most out of your day by visiting our amazing animal exhibits, talks, feeds and demonstrations.

## PASSAGE THROUGH ASIA

Drive your car or jump aboard our fantastic steam train and chug your way through the Passage Through Asia. Keep your eyes peeled for Indian rhinos, Asian elephants, camels and deer going about their daily business.

## FEEDING TIME

Whether it's delicious home-cooked food or a sandwich, coffee and a cake, we have several tasty options for you at the Zoo. Plus, all our food uses locally-sourced ingredients.

## SEALION SPLASH

Join our sealions as they show off their skills at Sealion Splash and get a unique chance to see them up close, but be warned – if you sit near the front, you will get wet!

## BIRDS OF THE WORLD

Take flight with our feathered friends and be ready to duck and dive as hawks, owls and macaws swoop over your head in this amazing Birds of the World demonstration.

## NEW GIRAFFE PLATFORM

See more than ever before of our family of reticulated giraffes. The nine-foot high platform will allow you to see across the entire giraffe paddock as well as provide a view into the indoor giraffe barn on chillier days.

## LOOKOUT LODGE

Spend the night at a sleepover like no other, where you see what happens in the Zoo after dark!

**1** Why has the writer used sub-headings in the text?
Give **two** reasons.

1. _____

2. _____

**2** What is the purpose of this text?

Tick **one**.

to explain and instruct ☐

to inform and entertain ☐

to entertain and persuade ☐

to persuade and inform ☐

**3** **Find** and **copy two** words or phrases that would tempt you to visit the zoo.

1. _____

2. _____

**4** What is the writer's opinion of the food on offer?

_____

_____

**5** Give **two** facts about the *giraffe platform*.

1. _____

2. _____

# Jacqueline Wilson at Christmas

These questions will help you practise:
★ retrieving and recording information
★ identifying key details
★ summarising main ideas
★ explaining the meaning of words in context
★ explaining how information contributes to meaning
★ making inferences.

## Film

My favourite is one of those movies that's always on at Christmas time – *The Wizard of Oz*. I first saw it as a child at my local cinema. It's an enchanting film, and I don't think anything beats the moment when Dorothy leaves colourless, grey Kansas and arrives in the wonderful world of Oz. I've got the DVD, but if it's on television I still jolly well have to watch it. It always puts me in a Christmassy mood.

## Book

My favourite book is a children's story, *Nancy and Plum*, by Betty MacDonald. It begins and ends at Christmas time and is about two little orphans who are having a terrible time in an orphanage, but by the end of the book have found a family and are having a fantastic Yuletide.

## Music

My favourite album is *The Cherry Tree*, a Christmas album by Anonymous 4, an American **a capella** group who sing medieval songs very beautifully. My favourite Christmas song is Lily Allen's version of Keane's *Somewhere Only We Know*, which featured in John Lewis' festive advert. I don't usually recognise a song unless it's been sung to death.

## Television

I'm a great animal lover and my favourite TV programme is Paul O'Grady's *For the Love Of Dogs*. It's set in Battersea Dogs and Cats Home, is very truthful and features such heart-warming stories, nearly all of which have happy endings. I've got two cats and a spirited little terrier called Jackson, all of which came from Battersea. The Home vets any potential owners particularly carefully at this time of the year, because as we all know, a dog is for life not just for Christmas.

## Theatre

I'm not one for pantos, but I've just seen a new adaptation of *The Lion, The Witch And The Wardrobe* – a story I always associate with the festive period. It looks Christmassy too, because there is snow in Narnia!

## Art

The painting I always try to see at Christmas is Geertgen tot Sint Jans's *The Nativity At Night* at the National Gallery. It shows a beautiful Madonna kneeling in front of Jesus, and is just a lovely picture.

### Glossary

- **a capella** singing without instruments

**1** From which country does the writer's favourite singing group come?

_____

1
(1 mark)

**2** The writer of the text loves Christmas.
Write **two** details to support this.

1. _____

2. _____

2
(2 marks)

**3** Match the heading to the idea presented in that paragraph.

| Film | | full of heart-warming stories |
| Book | | takes the writer into a wonderful world |
| Television | | starts sad but ends happily |
| Music | | a very familiar festive version |

3
(1 mark)

**4** In the paragraph about **_Television_** what does the word _spirited_ tell you about the dog?

_____

_____

4
(1 mark)

**5** What kind of text do you think this is?
Explain your answer, using evidence from the text.

_____

_____

5
(1 mark)

**6** **Find** and **copy two** phrases that are opinions.

1. _____

2. _____

6
(2 marks)

/ 8

Total for
this text

# The orang-utan nursery

These questions will help you practise:
★ making inferences
★ summarising main ideas
★ understanding words in context
★ retrieving and recording information
★ making predictions.

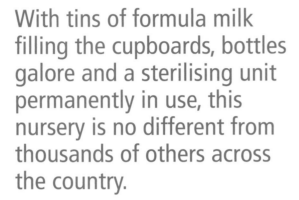

With tins of formula milk filling the cupboards, bottles galore and a sterilising unit permanently in use, this nursery is no different from thousands of others across the country.

Jars of Sudocrem for nappy rash are dotted about, there's a changing mat and plenty of fresh nappies. But as new mum Kate Diver nurses her little charge, gently winding him after a meal and rubbing Bonjela into his aching gums as he teethes, it's clear this is no ordinary baby.

Instead, Bulu Mata is an orphaned 12-week-old orang-utan, brought into Monkey World in Dorset earlier this month after his mother suddenly died from an intestine problem, a week after his birth in Budapest Zoo. The Head of Apes is one of a team of four staff currently nursing the little lad, whose name means 'long eyelashes' in Indonesian, round the clock.

But looking through the window with interest at this quaint scene is a far more important individual. It's Hsaio-qua, an 18-year-old orang-utan who's been at the rescue centre since she was abandoned outside a Taiwan amusement park aged five.

Staff hope she will soon take over their duties and become the baby ape's mum.

She's been chosen because her maternal instinct is so strong: she's had two sons of her own and, three years ago, adopted a tiny female called Awan, who had been abandoned by her mother.

As soon as she saw the baby's plight, she stepped in and swept the little one up into her arms. But now Awan is three-and-a-half and staff feel her adoptive mum is ready for another challenge. They've introduced them and Hsaio-qua showed some interest, touching and sniffing the new baby, but she's yet to pick him up and take him as her own like she did with Awan.

'We're really confident she will love Bulu Mata,' says the director of Monkey World. 'He's got everything he needs to bring out the nurturing instinct in her – huge eyes, cute little wriggles.'

Now seven pounds, he's already trying to push himself up to stand. To encourage him, staff regularly hold his fingers and help him 'walk' a few baby steps. It's vital he builds up his strength so that, when he is finally adopted, he can hold on tight to his new mum as she whirls around the trees, high above the ground, in her enclosure.

**1** Using information from the text, tick one box in each row to show whether each statement is a **fact** or an **opinion**.

|  | Fact | Opinion |
|---|---|---|
| Bulu Mata has teething pains. |  |  |
| Hsaio-qua will love Bulu Mata. |  |  |
| Bulu Mata means 'long eyelashes'. |  |  |
| Bulu Mata was born in Budapest. |  |  |
| Hsaio-qua is ready for another challenge. |  |  |

1
(2 marks)

**2** What is the most important thing this text tells you about Bulu Mata?

Tick **one**.

Bulu Mata is a baby orang-utan. ☐

Bulu Mata needs a new mother. ☐

Bulu Mata is teething. ☐

Bulu Mata is being cared for in a zoo. ☐

2
(1 mark)

**3** The word *nurturing* has been used to describe Hsaio-qua because she is…

Tick **one**.

old. ☐

caring. ☐

friendly. ☐

strong. ☐

3
(1 mark)

**4** What does Kate Driver use to help:

nappy rash? _____

aching gums? _____

4
(2 marks)

**5** What do you think will happen to Bulu Mata? Refer to the text in your answer.

_____

_____

_____

/ 8

Total for
this text

# The history of chocolate

These questions will help you practise:
* ★ retrieving and recording information
* ★ making inferences
* ★ explaining how information is related
* ★ summarising main ideas
* ★ explaining inferences.

Chocolate has been around for a lot longer than most people imagine, and dates back to almost 2000 years BC – but it wasn't always edible or sweet. Our chocolate bars and Easter eggs would look and taste unrecognisable to the original chocolate lovers.

**1900BC** Archaeological evidence shows that people drank chocolate in **Mesoamerica**.

**200AD–900AD** The Mayans. Cocoa was an important part of both their agriculture and religious life. On ceremonial and religious occasions they drank a spicy chocolate drink called xocoatl, made by grinding up cocoa beans then adding water and spices such as chilli. The Mayans also used cocoa beans as currency.

**900AD–1500AD** The Aztec culture became established in Mexico. The Aztecs worshipped the same gods as the Mayans and used xocoatl in much the same way. Spanish **conquistadors** noted that 100 cocoa beans could purchase a turkey and a canoe filled with fresh water!

**1502** Christopher Columbus introduced the cocoa bean to Spain, but drinking cocoa didn't catch on.

**1528** Cortez realised the economic possibilities of the cocoa bean and the Spanish begin to sweeten the cocoa drink, making it more popular than before.

**1600 onwards** Although the practice of drinking chocolate began to spread across Europe, the price ensured it was a limited treat for the rich.

**1700 onwards** Advancements in machinery during the Industrial Revolution meant that chocolate could be produced in larger quantities. By 1770 there were approximately 2000 'chocolate houses' (like present-day coffee shops) in London.

**1824** John Cadbury opened a shop in Birmingham selling cocoa and drinking chocolate which he prepared using a pestle and mortar.

**1847** Joseph Fry produced the first chocolate bar.

## Glossary

* **Mesoamerica** a region covering all of Central America and parts of North and South America
* **conquistadors** soldiers and explorers who conquered territory around the world from the 15th to the 17th centuries

**1** What did the Spanish do to cocoa to make it a more popular drink?

_____

1

(1 mark)

**2** Using information from the text, tick one box in each row to show whether each statement is a **fact** or an **opinion**.

|  | Fact | Opinion |
|---|---|---|
| Easter eggs today would be unfamiliar to original chocolate lovers. |  |  |
| The Aztecs and Mayans drank xocoatl. |  |  |
| Drinking chocolate was expensive. |  |  |
| There were 2000 chocolate houses in London by 1770. |  |  |

2

(1 mark)

**3** Explain how the organisation of the information about chocolate is effective.

_____

_____

3

(1 mark)

**4** What is the main idea of the text?

Tick **one**.

Everyone loves to drink chocolate. ☐

The Spanish discovered chocolate. ☐

Chocolate has been popular for centuries. ☐

The Mayans discovered chocolate in 200AD–900AD. ☐

4

(1 mark)

**5** Why do you think people weren't interested in cocoa when Columbus introduced it to Spain in 1502?
Refer to the text in your answer.

_____

_____

5

(2 marks)

# The 'walk to school' debate

These questions will help you practise:
* ★ summarising main ideas
* ★ making inferences
* ★ making predictions
* ★ identifying key details
* ★ making comparisons.

Fewer primary-age children walk to school now than ever before. Many children leave primary school never having made their own way to or from school. Health research suggests that walking could have an important role to play in the health of the nation. However, this needs to be balanced against concerns about children's safety.

There can be no doubt that regular walking aids physical wellbeing. Indeed, the latest government research shows that those taking regular exercise are more alert, efficient and less prone to daydreaming. Furthermore, schools involved in 'Walk to School' weeks have reported that children improve socially and get on better in school. Parents also think that children become more independent as they begin to deal with the world outside their home. Environmentalists also campaign in this area. They claim that as much as 30% of traffic on the road between 8:30 and 9:00 is due to parents making short journeys to school. If children walked to school, traffic would be reduced. Roads would therefore be safer and the air cleaner.

On the other hand, many would say that walking without adult supervision often puts children at risk. In busy modern life, it is not often practical for adults to spend their time walking children to school before rushing off to work. In any case, children are taking exercise in clubs and after-school classes in a safe, supervised environment.

While acknowledging the environmentalists' concerns, other research suggests that short car trips to school are insignificant in the battle against pollution. Other sources of pollution should be looked at before this one.

There is clearly an issue of child safety in the 'Walk to School' debate, however the arguments for walking to school remain strong. Ways of ensuring walking is supervised (perhaps by adults on a rota) should be explored. The health of children will only be improved if they exercise at every opportunity.

**1** What is the purpose of the *'Walk to School' debate*?

Tick **one**.

to persuade ☐

to inform ☐

to discuss ☐

to instruct ☐

**2** Using information from the text, tick one box in each row to show whether each statement is a **fact** or an **opinion**.

| | Fact | Opinion |
|---|---|---|
| Few primary-age children walk to school. | | |
| Parents make short car journeys to school. | | |
| Short car trips don't cause much pollution. | | |
| Children are at risk from walking to school. | | |

**3** What could happen to the environment if the traffic on the road increases between 8:30 and 9:00 a.m.?

_____

_____

**4** Give **two** benefits of **walking** to school, compared to driving to school.

1. _____

2. _____

**5** Give **two** benefits of **driving** to school, compared to walking to school.

1. _____

2. _____

# The sound collector

These questions will help you practise:
* ★ explaining how language choices enhance meaning
* ★ explaining the meaning of words in context
* ★ identifying how information is related
* ★ explaining inferences.

A stranger called this morning
Dressed all in black and grey
Put every sound into a bag
And carried them away

The whistling of the kettle
The turning of the lock
The purring of the kitten
The ticking of the clock

The popping of the toaster
The crunching of the flakes
When you spread the marmalade
The scraping noise it makes

The hissing of the frying-pan
The ticking of the grill
The bubbling of the bathtub
As it starts to fill

The drumming of the raindrops
On the window-pane
When you do the washing-up
The gurgle of the drain

The crying of the baby
The squeaking of the chair
The swishing of the curtain
The creaking of the stair

A stranger called this morning
He didn't leave his name
Left us only silence
Life will never be the same.

Roger McGough

**1** What is the main effect the writer has used in this poem?

Tick **one**.

simile ☐

alliteration ☐

onomatopoeia ☐

metaphor ☐

☐ 1
(1 mark)

**2** *The drumming of the raindrops.*

What does the word *drumming* tell us about the rain?

_____

_____

☐ 2
(1 mark)

**3** **Find** and **copy** the only example of **alliteration** in this poem.

_____

☐ 3
(1 mark)

**4** The poem has a strong rhythm.
What effect does this have?

_____

_____

☐ 4
(1 mark)

**5** **Find** and **copy** the line in the poem that is repeated.

_____

☐ 5
(1 mark)

**6** Look at the last line of the poem.
Explain why *life will never be the same.*

_____

_____

☐ 6
(1 mark)

/ 6
Total for
this text

45

# The reader of this poem

These questions will help you practise:
★ identifying and explaining how language choices enhance meaning
★ explaining how information contributes to meaning
★ explaining inferences
★ retrieving and recording information.

1  The reader of this poem
   Is as cracked as a cup
   As daft as a treacle-toffee
   As mucky as a pup

2  As troublesome as bubblegum
   As brash as a brush
   As bouncy as a double-tum
   As quiet as a sshhh…

3  As sneaky as a witch's spell
   As tappytoe as jazz
   As empty as a wishing-well
   As echoey as as as as as as…

4  As bossy as a whistle
   As prickly as a pair
   Of boots made out of thistles
   And elephant hair

5  As vain as trainers
   As boring as a draw
   As smelly as a drain is
   Outside the kitchen door

6  As hungry as a wave
   That feeds upon the coast
   As gaping as the grave
   As GOTCHA! as a ghost

7  As fruitless as a cake of soap
   As creeping-up as smoke
   The reader of this poem, I hope
   Knows how to take a joke!

   Roger McGough

46

**1** What is the effect of writing *As echoey as as as as as as…?*

_____

_____

**2** Why is the word *GOTCHA* written in capital letters?

_____

_____

**3** Match the words to complete phrases from the poem.

| cracked | | as a whistle |
| brash | | as a cup |
| hungry | | as a brush |
| bossy | | as a wave |

**4** a) The writer uses many **similes** in this poem.
   **Find** and **copy one**.

_____

b) Explain the effect of the simile you have chosen.

_____

_____

**5** *The reader of this poem, I hope*
*Knows how to take a joke!*

Why do you think the writer chose to end the poem this way?

_____

_____

_____

_____

_____

# Pumpkin for Maxine

These questions will help you practise:
* ★ identifying how language choices enhance meaning
* ★ identifying how information contributes to meaning
* ★ explaining the meaning of words in context
* ★ identifying key details
* ★ explaining inferences.

On Hallowe'en Mum and I made a pumpkin lantern;
huge triangular eyes and a square nose.
It cried when we dug out its pyramid teeth:
*Ouch, it said, this is worse than the dentist.*
I got a fright; but the strangest thing was,
my mum didn't hear it. *Dentists at least give gas*,
Pumpkin complained. There was my mum, oblivious,
still hacking out its brain. 'Come on. Dig in,' she says,
'this is taking hours; it'll turn back into a carriage.'
I started feeling dizzy, giddy, all out of sorts.
I tried to hold its jaw closed so it couldn't talk.
*Ouch, it said, my cheekbone; do I have to be hollow?*
'Of course you do,' I whispered, 'this is all hallow's
eve. We will put a candle in the hollow.' *Oh no*,
screamed Pumpkin. *I'm going to burn, my skull.*
*Worse than Catherine.* Suddenly, Pumpkin rolled
off the table. 'Look what you've done!' shouted Mum.
'You careless thing.' 'It wasn't me,' I said breathless,
and pleased. Pumpkin was trying to escape.
'Oh, for goodness' sake,' said Mum.
'What's the matter with your head?'
*It's not her head*, Pumpkin said, *It's mine.*
*I've got a dreadful headache, got anything for it?*
But my mum, who'd suddenly, finally heard it –
Pumpkin's piercing voice – fainted, falling
into the basin with all the apples for the **dooking**.

Jackie Kay

**Glossary**
* **dooking** dunking

**1** **Find** and **copy** an example of personification in the poem.

_____

**2** What is the purpose of the **italics** in the poem?
Give **one** purpose.

_____

**3** *There was my mum, oblivious, still hacking out its brain.*

Explain why the word *oblivious* is a suitable word to use in this sentence.

_____

**4** The writer of the poem suggests that the pumpkin could feel pain.
Give **two** details to support this idea.

1.  _____

2.  _____

**5** Explain how the writer feels about hollowing out the pumpkin.
Explain fully, referring to the text in your answer.

_____
_____
_____
_____
_____

# Me and my brother

These questions will help you practise:
* ★ identifying how information is related
* ★ explaining how information contributes to meaning
* ★ summarising main ideas
* ★ explaining inferences
* ★ making predictions
* ★ retrieving information.

Me and my brother,
we sit up in bed
doing my dad's sayings.
I go to bed first
and I'm just dozing off
and I hear a funny voice going:
'Never let me see you doing that again,'
and it's my brother
poking his finger out just like my dad
going:
'Never let me see you doing that again.'
And so I join in
and we're both going:
'Never let me see you doing that again.'
So what happens next time when we get into
    trouble
and my dad's telling me off?
He's going:
'Never let me see you doing that again.'
So I'm looking up at my dad going,
'Sorry, Dad, sorry,'
and I suddenly catch sight of my brother's
big red face
poking out from behind my dad.
And while my dad is poking me with his
    finger in time with the words:
'Never let me see you doing that again,'
there's my brother doing just the same
behind my dad's back
just where I can see him
and he's saying the words as well

with his mouth without making a sound.
So I start laughing
and my dad says,
'AND IT'S NO LAUGHING MATTER.'
Of course my brother knows that one as well
and he's going with his mouth:
'And it's no laughing matter.'
But my dad's not stupid.
He knows something's going on.
So he looks round
and there's my brother
with his finger poking out
just like my dad
and I'm standing there laughing.
Oh no
then we get into
REALLY BIG TROUBLE.

Michael Rosen

**1** How has this poem been organised?

Tick **one**.

by repeating words that rhyme ☐

like a story ☐

as a conversation ☐

in the style of a song ☐

☐ 1
(1 mark)

**2** How does the writer build a picture of the characters of the children?

_____

_____

☐ 2
(1 mark)

**3** Why are the words _AND IT'S NO LAUGHING MATTER_ written in **capitals**?

_____

_____

☐ 3
(1 mark)

**4** Why do you think the writer laughed when his dad was telling him off?

_____

☐ 4
(1 mark)

**5** What is the main idea in this poem?

_____

_____

☐ 5
(1 mark)

**6** What do you think Dad might say next in the poem?
Give **two** suggestions.

1. _____

2. _____

☐ 6
(2 marks)

**7** The writer's brother is...

Tick **one**.

good at imitating people. ☐

good at apologising. ☐

a good brother. ☐

a good son. ☐

☐ 7
(1 mark)

/ 8

_Total for
this text_

51

# Silver

These questions will help you practise:
- ★ identifying and explaining how language choices enhance meaning
- ★ giving the meaning of words in context
- ★ explaining how information contributes to meaning
- ★ summarising main ideas.

Slowly, silently, now the moon

Walks the night in her silver **shoon**;

This way, and that, she peers, and sees

Silver fruit upon silver trees;

One by one the **casements** catch

Her beams beneath the silvery thatch;

Crouched in his kennel, like a log,

With paws of silver sleeps the dog;

From their shadowy cote the white breasts peep

Of doves in a silver-feathered sleep;

A harvest mouse goes scampering by,

With silver claws, and silver eye;

And moveless fish in the water gleam,

By silver reeds in a silver stream.

Walter de la Mare

### Glossary
- **shoon** shoes
- **casements** windowpanes

52

**1** **Find** and **copy** an example of personification in the poem.

_____

1
(1 mark)

**2** _Silver fruit upon silver trees;_

Why does the writer use the word _silver_ to describe the trees and the fruit?

_____

_____

2
(1 mark)

**3** _From their shadowy cote the white breasts peep_

_Of doves in a silver-feathered sleep;_

What does the word _cote_ mean in this phrase?

_____

3
(1 mark)

**4** Explain how the writer gives the impression of _stillness_ throughout the night.

_____
_____
_____
_____
_____

4
(3 marks)

**5** Write **one** sentence explaining the main idea in this poem.

_____

5
(1 mark)

/ 7

Total for
this text

# The centipede's song

These questions will help you practise:
★ retrieving and recording information
★ explaining how information contributes to meaning
★ identifying how language choices enhance meaning
★ summarising main ideas
★ making inferences.

'I've eaten many strange and scrumptious dishes in my time,

Like jellied gnats and dandyprats and earwigs cooked in slime,

And mice with rice – they're really nice

When roasted in their prime.

(But don't forget to sprinkle them with just a pinch of grime.)


'I've eaten fresh mudburgers by the greatest cooks there are,

And scrambled dregs and stinkbugs' eggs and hornets

stewed in tar,

And pails of snails and lizards' tails,

And beetles by the jar.

(A beetle is improved by just a splash of vinegar.)


'I often eat boiled slobbages. They're grand when served beside

Minced doodlebugs and curried slugs. And have you ever tried

Mosquitoes' toes and wampfish roes most delicately fried?

(The only trouble is they disagree with my inside.)

From *James and the Giant Peach* by Roald Dahl

**1**  Match the groups of food that were eaten together.

| mice | | lizards' tails |
|---|---|---|
| minced doodlebugs | | curried slugs |
| scrambled dregs | | rice |
| snails | | hornets stewed in tar |

**2**  Explain the purpose of the brackets at the end of each verse.

_____

_____

_____

**3**  How does the writer create a sense of humour in the poem?
Give **two** details to support your answer.

1.  _____

2.  _____

**4**  Write **one** sentence to summarise the main idea in this poem.

_____

**5**  What other kinds of food do you think the narrator of the poem would enjoy?
Refer to the text in your answer.

_____

_____

_____

_____

_____